Tell

Norah McClintock

orca soundings

Orca Book Publishers

Library and Archives Canada Cataloguing in Publication

McClintock, Norah

Tell / Norah McClintock.

(Orca Soundings)
ISBN 1-55143-672-8 (bound) ISBN 1-55143-511-X (pbk.)

PS8575.C62T44 2006   jC813'.54   C2006-903260-2

Summary: When David's stepfather is murdered, he knows
more than he is telling.

First published in the United States, 2006
Library of Congress Control Number: 2006928470

Orca Book Publishers gratefully acknowledges the support for its publishing
programs provided by the following agencies: the Government of Canada
through the Book Publishing Industry Development Program and the
Canada Council for the Arts, and the Province of British Columbia
through the BC Arts Council and the Book Publishing Tax Credit.

Cover design: Doug McCaffry
Cover photography: Firstlight

Orca Book Publishers
PO Box 5626 Station B
Victoria, BC Canada
V8R 6S4

Orca Book Publishers
PO Box 468
Custer, WA USA
98240-0468

www.orcabook.com

Printed and bound in Canada

09 08 07 06 • 5 4 3 2 1

To Willie and the rest of them

Chapter One

It was Saturday night when the cops came to our house. Actually, it was 2:00 AM, so technically that made it Sunday morning. The doorbell rang twice before I heard my mother's slippered feet shuffling along the upstairs hall and down the stairs. I pressed the mute button on the TV remote and listened through my bedroom door to muffled voices in the front hall below. I heard my mother wail. It was a terrible sound, like an animal being tortured.

Her voice got higher and higher and she said, "No, no, no" over and over, louder and louder. I got up off my bed and went downstairs.

There were two people in the front hall. They were cops. One of them was a woman. She was trying to steer my mother into the living room where she could sit down. My mother was crying. She kept saying, "I don't know what I'm going to do without him."

"Mom?" I said. "What's wrong? What's the matter?"

The two cops looked at me. The female cop managed to get my mother seated on the couch in the living room. The male cop introduced himself. "I'm Detective Antonelli," he said. "I'm afraid we have some bad news." He paused and looked at me.

"David," I said. "I'm David."

"We have some bad news, David. It's about your father."

"You mean Phil?" I said. Detective Antonelli gave me a look. "He's not my father," I said. "He's my stepfather."

Then, because I knew how it would look if I didn't ask, I said, "Is he okay? Did he do something?"

My mother was sobbing in the living room.

Detective Antonelli pulled me aside. When he spoke, he kept his voice low.

"Is there anyone else in the house, David? Do you have any brothers or sisters? Any other relatives staying with you?"

I shook my head.

"What happened?" I said. "Where's Phil?"

"I'm afraid he was shot and killed a couple of hours ago," Detective Antonelli said.

"*What?*" I said. "How? Why?"

"We're not sure about all the details. It looks like it might have been a robbery." He was looking closely at me now, probably because it was so late and I was still wearing jeans and a T-shirt, not pajamas. "Did you just get home, David?"

"I was watching TV up in my room," I said. "I guess I fell asleep." I turned to look at my mother in the living room. The woman cop was talking quietly to her. My mother was shaking her head and moaning softly. I looked at Detective Antonelli again. "I should see how my mom is," I said.

"I'd like to ask you a few questions first, if that's okay," Detective Antonelli said. He was talking softly and being polite. But I had the feeling that he would ask his questions even if I said it wasn't okay. "Why don't we step in here?" he said. He nodded toward the dining room, which was across the hall from the living room.

We went inside and sat down at the dining room table.

"When was the last time you saw your stepfather?" he said.

"What?" I don't know what I had been expecting him to ask me, but it sure wasn't that.

"I mean, was he home today?"

"Yes," I said.

"But he went out at some point?" Detective Antonelli said.

"He left right after supper," I said. "He went to play poker with some friends."

"Do you know where?"

"At Jack's place," I said. I explained that Jack Tower was a friend of Phil's.

"What about you and your mother?"

I stared at him. Why was he asking about us?

"Was your mother home all night?" he said.

"Yes," I said.

"Were you home with her?"

I had to fight the urge to turn to look at my mother again.

"I was out for a couple of hours," I said.

"Where did you go?"

I shrugged. "Just out, you know? Walking around."

"Were you with friends?"

Geez, why was he asking about me?

"No," I said. "I just like to walk around. I think better when I'm walking."

He kept staring at me, like he was waiting for me to say more.

"I write comic books," I said. "With a friend of mine. He draws the pictures and I write the stories. I was trying to think up a new story."

"When exactly were you out?" he said.

"I left the house around 8:00," I said. My mother would be able to back me up on that. "I got back around 10:30." My mother had been asleep in bed when I got home. Based on past experience and on the fact that she'd been on her feet from 8:00 in the morning until 5:00 at the supermarket where she worked as a cashier and then had made supper for Phil and me when she got home, I figured she must have crashed out around 9:00. She wouldn't be able to tell anyone for sure exactly when I had got home. "Why?" I said. "You don't think my mother had anything to do with it, do you?"

"We're trying to trace your stepfather's movements this evening, David."

"But you said it was a robbery," I said.

"It looks like it might have been a robbery," Detective Antonelli said carefully. "He was found about half a block from an ATM machine. We have reason to believe that he had just withdrawn some money."

"Then probably someone saw him take out the money and robbed him," I said. "You hear about stuff like that happening all the time."

Detective Antonelli's expression was impossible to read.

"We didn't find a wallet," he said. "We identified him from a utility bill that he had in one of his pockets. We didn't find any keys, either. Does your stepfather have a car?"

I nodded.

"Did he take it when he went out tonight?"

"Yes."

He asked me about the car. I described it and gave him the license plate number. Then he asked me about Jack. I gave him Jack's address and phone number.

"You don't think Jack shot him, do you?"

He didn't answer the question directly. He just said, "We like to be thorough."

Across the hall, my mother was still quietly sobbing.

"I should see how she is," I said.

Detective Antonelli nodded. I went into the living room, sat down on the couch beside my mother and put my arm around her. She sagged against me, still crying.

"It's going to be okay," I told her. I sure hoped I was right.

Chapter Two

A parade of people came to the house all day to tell my mother how sorry they were about what had happened and to drop off food. They drank so much coffee that my mother sent me to the store to buy more. When I got back, I found her in tears— again. She was crying this time because Detective Antonelli had telephoned her and asked her to come down to the police station to answer some more questions about Phil.

"I'll go with you," I said. I figured it was the least I could do.

"We found your husband's car," Detective Antonelli said after he had showed us into a small interview room. "It was parked up the street from where he was found. We also found his wallet and keys. I know this must be hard for you, Mrs. Benson, but it would really help us if you would take a look at his personal effects and tell us if anything is missing."

My mother agreed, of course.

Phil's personal effects were:

(1) His wallet, which had been emptied of money, but which still contained his credit cards and his ID. Also inside the wallet was a picture of my mother. She was wearing shorts and a tank top, and she looked nervous sitting at the end of a dock. There was a cottage in the background.

(2) His watch, which was about ten years old and was nothing special. It had a leather strap. It wasn't hard to figure out why whoever had killed him hadn't bothered to take it.

(3) His wedding ring. It was a plain gold band and was engraved on the inside with his initials and my mother's initials.

(4) A slip from an ATM machine that showed he had withdrawn five hundred dollars on Saturday night.

(5) A brand-new deck of playing cards. The seal hadn't been broken.

(6) A lighter and two cigars. Phil liked to smoke cigars when he was driving or when he was playing poker at one of his buddies' places—if the buddy's wife or girlfriend allowed it.

(7) A key-ring chain with a fake-gold letter *P* attached to it, along with his house keys and car keys.

"We found the keys a couple of blocks from where we found the wallet. They were both found in opposite directions from the car," Detective Antonelli said. He frowned, as if this was some kind of problem. "Maybe whoever robbed him planned to take the car but changed his mind. Maybe he couldn't find the car. Or maybe he didn't see your husband drive up, so he didn't know that he had a car with him."

My mother's eyes widened. "Do you think that whoever killed Phil saw where we live, you know, from the driver's license in the wallet? Do you think he's planning to break into the house while we're at the funeral? I've heard that people do that. They rob the houses of people who are already grieving."

"I think if that were the case, he would have kept the keys," Detective Antonelli said.

My mother continued to look worried. She stared at Phil's key ring and started to cry again.

Detective Antonelli nudged a box of tissues closer to her.

"Is there anything that you can think of that might be missing?" he said.

My mother nodded as she wiped at her tears with a tissue. She blew her nose.

"The picture of Jamie," she said. Jamie was my kid brother. "Phil always has a picture of Jamie with him." I wondered if she noticed that she had said "has" instead of "had," as if Phil was still alive.

"Jamie?" Detective Antonelli said.

"My other son," my mother said. She got all choked up again as she explained that Jamie had drowned when he was eight years old. That was nearly six years ago now, when I had just turned ten.

"Phil has a picture of him," she said. "It's in a little gold frame attached to his key chain. He says he carries it because he never wants to forget Jamie."

Me, I was the opposite. I wished I could forget what had happened, but I couldn't. Instead I had replayed every detail of it in my mind every night for a couple of years. I still saw it a few times a month, like a movie, as clearly as if it were yesterday.

"Where is it?" my mother said. "Where's the picture of Jamie?"

Detective Antonelli frowned again. "Whoever took the keys may have taken the frame. Is it real gold?"

My mother nodded. "I bought it for him."

"Well, maybe that's why the thief took it," Detective Antonelli said. He asked my mother one last time if there was anything else missing. When she said no, he thanked us for coming in.

I stayed home from school on Monday. More people phoned and came to the house. Later, I changed into a sports jacket, a good pair of pants (not jeans), a shirt with a tie (I had to borrow one of Phil's), and regular shoes, not sneakers. My mother changed into a black skirt and a black top. She didn't want to drive, which was probably a good thing because she kept crying, so we took a taxi to the funeral home for the viewing. My mother made me go with her to look at Phil, who was lying in a casket in his best suit. She stood there for a long time, staring at him, kissing him on the cheek a couple of times (don't ask me how she could make herself do that) and crying. After a while, we sat down facing the coffin. Jack was there, dressed in a dark suit. He shook hands with everyone who came to look at Phil and to hug my mother. He thanked everyone for coming.

Every time someone came up to my mother to tell her how sorry they were about Phil, she turned on the waterworks. I thought she would dry out, she was crying so much.

People said the same things to me that they said to her: *I'm sorry for your loss. I can't imagine how you must feel, losing your father. He was such a great guy.*

"I wish people would stop calling him that," I complained to my mother later, when almost everyone had left.

"Stop calling him what?" she said.

"My father. Phil wasn't my father."

"He raised you from when you were eight," she said.

"But he wasn't my father."

"Stop saying that," my mother said. She was angry now and tears were gathering in her eyes. "I don't know what I would have done if I hadn't met him. I don't know how I would have managed to raise two boys on my own. Don't you remember what it was like, David? Don't you remember how hard it was before Phil came along?"

Before Phil, my mother had been on welfare. We lived in a rundown apartment that had mice and cockroaches, leaky pipes, broken tiles in the bathroom, no air-conditioning, and elevators that never worked. I remember my mother used to cry all the time then too because there was never enough money and she never got a break from looking after Jamie and me.

"Phil took good care of us," she said and burst into tears again.

I put my arms around her until she calmed down. I handed her some tissues, and she dried her eyes. I told her again that everything was going to be all right.

Chapter Three

I thought the viewing was bad. The funeral the next morning was worse. My mother didn't just cry. She sobbed. Especially when Jack got up and spoke about Phil.

Jack is a good guy, which is why I always had a hard time figuring out why he hung out with Phil. They played poker together almost every weekend, and every fall Jack and Phil and a couple of other guys went on a hunting trip together.

After Jack spoke, a guy from Phil's work, a trucker like Phil, got up. He said that Phil was a devoted family man and that he always talked about his family when he was away from home, which was basically from Monday to Friday, when he hauled a load of something halfway across the continent and a load of something else all the way back again. He said that Phil talked about his wife all the time—and my mother started to bawl. He said that Phil always treated his two stepsons like they were his own flesh and blood, and he described how broken up Phil had been when the younger one drowned. He said that Phil carried a picture of Jamie on his key chain, that it was always right in front of him, dangling from his ignition, and that he'd lay it on the bar next to him after he finished driving for the day and was ready to hoist a cold one. He said that Phil was always telling people about Jamie and his other son, David. He said that's the way he referred to me—as his son, not his stepson. He said Phil was proud of me.

Yeah. Right.

My mother was practically hysterical when they got ready to close the coffin. For a minute there, I thought she was going to crawl inside with Phil. She was sobbing and moaning. Tears were rushing down her cheeks. She was holding a wad of tissues that was all wet and clumpy from all the crying she had done. Jack had to hold onto her to keep her on her feet.

From the church we went to the cemetery, where my mother cried some more. Then we all went back to our house, where a bunch of my mother's friends were waiting with food for all the guests. After that it was kind of like a party—people talked about a lot of things besides Phil. My mother sat on the couch in the living room with a couple of her friends. She was pale and looked tired.

"Tough day, huh, David?" Jack said. He had come outside on the back porch where I was sitting. He dropped down onto the top step beside me and took a swallow from the beer bottle in his hand. "How are you holding up?"

"Okay, I guess," I said. "I'm kind of worried about Mom, though. She hasn't stopped crying in days."

"It's scary for her," Jack said. "She's afraid to be on her own."

"She's not on her own," I said. "I'm here."

Jack squeezed my shoulder. "I know, David. What I meant is, she's afraid to be on her own with no one to look after her the way Phil did. Maybe she's afraid she's going to end up the way she did after your dad went away."

I looked at him. That was a funny way to put it. *After your dad went away,* like he'd taken a trip instead of died.

When Jack looked back at me, something changed in his face. He took a quick gulp of beer and stared out at our backyard, which was more weeds than grass. Phil always said that he worked hard all week, so he damn sure wasn't going to work like a farmer all weekend, trying to grow Astroturf in his backyard the way all the neighbors did. My mother wasn't interested in gardening either, other than sending me next door to borrow the Taylors' lawn mower every so often and getting me to run it over what grass was out there.

"What I meant was," Jack said again, "it was hard on your mother when she was alone with you and Jamie. She worried all the time. She stopped worrying after she met Phil."

That wasn't exactly true. If you ask me, she just worried about different things. Mostly she worried that Jamie or me or both of us would do something to make Phil think that going out with a woman who already had two kids was a bad idea. Jamie was five years old when Mom started seeing Phil. I was seven. When Phil used to come over, when they were still just going out, she used to bribe us to be good (*I'll rent you some games for your PlayStation*) or threaten us (*If I have to tell you even once to be quiet or to behave, there'll be no TV for a week—I mean it, boys*). I mostly listened, but not Jamie. Jamie never listened to anyone, ever. When I think about it now, I think maybe he was one of those hyperactive kids, you know, the kind who can't sit still even if they wanted to.

Mom married Phil when Jamie was six and I was eight. After that she worried that Phil wouldn't stay married to her on account of us. She read somewhere that kids from a first marriage sink something like half of all second marriages. She told us, *If Phil tells you to do something, do it.* She said, *He's your father now.* She said, *If you mess up this relationship for me, I don't know what I'll do.* I didn't want to mess things up for her. I don't think Jamie did, either. But that didn't mean he could all of a sudden change into a different person.

Mom tried threatening him. She tried bribing him. Then she came up with an idea. He could be as wild as he wanted during the week, when Phil was on the road. But on weekends, when Phil was around, he had to be quiet and sit still and not make noise. Plus, he had to pay attention to Phil and do what Phil told him.

It was a bad plan. If you let a little kid like Jamie act any way he wants five days a week, he's just naturally going to want to act that way all the time. He got wilder and wilder. It really pissed Phil off on Friday nights when he got home, tired. And on Saturday morning, when he wanted to sleep in. And on Saturday afternoon, when he wanted to relax. And on Saturday night, when he and Jack and his other friends came over to play poker. And on Sunday morning, when he was hungover and wanted to sleep in again. And on Sunday afternoon, when he wanted to relax because first thing Monday morning he had to be on the road again.

So my mother worried about that. She worried all the time. I think she worried more after she married Phil than she did when she was raising us alone.

"Sometimes I think about my real dad," I said to Jack. "I wonder what he was like. I wish I remembered him."

Jack looked at me, surprised. "You do?" he said. "You never talk about him?"

"That's because Mom never wants to talk about him. But he must have been really smart. And I bet he was way nicer than Phil."

"You didn't like Phil much, did you, David?"

I looked down at the toes of my shoes. It didn't seem right to say you didn't like someone when you had just come from his funeral.

"Well, no matter what you think of him, Phil loved your mother," Jack said. "And he stuck around—even if he could be a jerk sometimes."

I was surprised to hear him say that. "I thought Phil was your friend," I said.

"We played poker," Jack said with a shrug.

He made it sound like things hadn't been the way I thought, like he and Phil weren't best buddies after all.

"I'm more a friend of your mom's than I was of Phil's," he said. "I've known your mom for a long time. I only met Phil because of her." That was news to me.

"She's stronger than she thinks, David. She's going to be okay."

"How long have you known Mom?" I said.

"Since high school."

That was news to me too.

"Did you know my dad?" I said.

Jack looked at me for a minute. I think he was going to tell me something. But someone started yelling in the house. It was my mother. She was all hysterical again when we got inside.

"He lied to me," she was saying. "He told me I would always be looked after, but he lied to me."

It took Jack a few minutes to find out what had happened. Phil had told my mother that he had life insurance and that if anything ever happened to him, she would have nothing to worry about. It turned out that wasn't true. He didn't have any insurance.

Chapter Four

The next day my mother started checking out other stuff about Phil. What she found made her mad at first and then started her crying again. It turned out Phil had a big mortgage on the house that my mother didn't know about. It was a new one. One of Phil's poker buddies told her later that Phil had taken out the mortgage because he gambled a lot and lost a lot. It also turned out that there was almost nothing in the bank.

"We're not going to be able to stay in this house," she told me that night. Her eyes were all red and puffy, but she wasn't crying anymore. "I can't afford the mortgage payments on what I make at the supermarket. Even if I get more hours, it still won't be enough for the mortgage and all the bills."

"Where will we go?" I said.

"If we sell the house, we'll make some money. Not a lot, but some. And we can probably sell some of the furniture and some of Phil's things. We'll find an apartment. A *nice* apartment, not like that one we were in before. I'm going to see about getting more hours and maybe even another job. I think you're going to have to find an after-school and weekend job, David. We're going to be on a pretty tight budget."

I stared at her.

"What's the matter?" she said. "Why are you looking at me like that?"

I got up and hugged her. "We're going to be okay, Mom. I know we are."

She hugged me back. "I don't know what I'd do without you. I love you, David."

I felt good about that.

When I got home from school the next day, my mother didn't act like she loved me. She was too busy freaking out.

"Where did you get this?" she screamed at me, shoving a hand into my face.

I couldn't understand what she was talking about. Where did I get *what*?

She opened her hand. In it was a small gold picture frame with a little loop in the corner of the frame. Usually there was a chain through the loop where you could attach it to a key ring. But there was no chain there now. It was broken off. In the frame was a picture of my kid brother.

"Where did you get this?" my mother screamed at me again.

I couldn't believe she had it in her hand. I had to force myself to stay calm. Instead of answering her question, I said, "Where did *you* get it, Mom?"

"I was doing the laundry. *Your* laundry."

Geez, most of the time she was nagging at me to put my dirty clothes in the hamper or was complaining because I was old enough to be doing my own laundry, so why was she still picking up after me and folding my stuff out of the dryer and putting it away? For the past few months, her rule had been that if I didn't at least make the effort to put it in the hamper, she wasn't going to make the effort to wash it. Then I could see what it felt like to wake up one morning and have nothing but dirty clothes to put on for school. So why all of a sudden was she picking up after me again and doing my laundry for me?

"I found this in the dryer," she said, still holding out the gold-framed picture. "You want to tell me how it got there, David?"

"I don't know, Mom," I said. "It looks like the chain got broken somehow. Maybe that's why the cops didn't find it with Phil's keys. Maybe it got broken and he put it in his pocket."

My mother stared at the broken end of the chain.

"There were some of Phil's things in the dryer from before," she said slowly. She didn't come right out and say before what.

"There you go," I said. "You know what probably happened? The chain broke and Phil put the picture in his pocket so he wouldn't lose it. But he forgot it was there when he put his pants in the wash. And you didn't notice." It sounded like something that really could have happened. "When you took Phil's stuff out of the dryer and put my stuff in—which, by the way, Mom, you didn't have to do, you know—you probably didn't see it there. You didn't see it until you took my stuff out."

I could see she was thinking it over.

"I guess you're right," she said at last. I couldn't tell for sure if she was convinced or not. But what other explanation could she come up with? After all, it wasn't like my prints were on the frame or the glass or anything.

Jack rang the doorbell at 6:00 that night. When I opened the door, he was standing on the porch with two big brown paper bags.

"I brought supper," he said. "I figured your mother wouldn't feel much like cooking."

When Jack walked into the kitchen with the bags, my mother smiled. I hadn't seen her do that in days. Then, when she saw what was in the bags, she started to cry. I glanced at Jack. But before I could ask my mother what was wrong, she threw her arms around Jack and hugged him and said, "Thank you." She looked down at what she was wearing—an old T-shirt and some sweatpants—and said, "Oh my God, I'm a mess."

"You look terrific, Melanie," Jack said. "Like always."

He was right. My mother was nice-looking. She was small and slim and she looked after herself. She said that was important. She said a man didn't want to come home after being away all week and see his wife looking like a hag.

"Just let me run up and change," she said. "David, you can set the table."

While she was upstairs, I looked in the bags that Jack had brought. The containers told me right away that we were having Chinese food for supper. That explained my mother's reaction. She loved Chinese food. But we only ever ordered take-out when Phil was home and could pay for it, and Phil didn't like Chinese food. He didn't like Indian or Thai or Japanese food either. "I like to know what I'm eating," he always said. He said he didn't trust people who served food all chopped up into little pieces and covered with sauce so that you couldn't tell right away what was on your plate. Needless to say, he never took my mother to a Chinese restaurant. He always went for steak houses or, better yet, bars and pubs where he could drink plenty of beer with his wings or his chicken fingers.

When my mother came back downstairs, she had taken her hair out of the ponytail she had been wearing. Now it hung down to her shoulders in waves. She had put on some makeup and had changed into a sleeveless top and a pair of tight-fitting black pants. She looked great, even if she was my mother. She opened a couple of beers for Jack and herself, and we ate fried rice and egg rolls, chicken balls and little spareribs, beef with broccoli, and chicken with cashews. It was all great.

After we finished eating, Jack made coffee for my mother and told her to go and relax. He and I cleaned up the kitchen. While he gathered up all the empty containers, I said, "You never answered my question."

"What question?" Jack said.

"About my dad. I asked you if you knew him, but you never answered."

"Why are you so interested in that all of a sudden?" Jack said.

I shrugged. "I always thought you were Phil's friend. I didn't know you'd known Mom for so long. So *did* you know him too? Did you know my dad?"

Jack glanced toward the living room, where my mother was sitting with her coffee. We could hear the TV. She was watching *Wheel of Fortune*, which she loved because she was pretty good at figuring out the puzzles before the contestants did.

"Yeah," he said this time. "I knew him."

"What was he like?"

Jack hesitated. He looked around, as if he was checking to see if we were alone.

"I probably shouldn't tell you this, David," he said. "It's none of my business. But if someone asks me a question, I'm not going to lie. That's not the kind of person I am. You understand?"

I said I did.

We went out onto the back porch and Jack closed the door. We sat on the steps and he started talking—about my dad. When he was finished, I didn't know what to say.

"Listen, David," Jack said. "I know you're probably going to want to talk to your mother about this. But maybe this isn't the right time, what with Phil dying and everything. I think maybe you should wait a while, okay?"

"Okay," I said, even though I felt like I was bursting.

Jack stuck around for a while after we finished cleaning up, and we played a couple of rounds of Yahtzee. My mother smiled all night. After he left, I couldn't stay quiet, no matter what I had promised Jack.

"I wish my real father was still alive," I told her. "Things would really have been different for us, wouldn't they, Mom?"

My mother looked at me, surprised, I think, that I'd mentioned him.

"Tell me about him, Mom," I said.

One hand went to her hair, which was dyed blond and which she wore down to her shoulders because Phil liked blonds and he loved long hair. She tucked it behind her ear and fiddled with the ends of it. It was the kind of thing a shy kid would do.

"What's there to tell, David?" she said. "You already know everything."

"I know," I said. "I just thought—it's just the two of us now, Mom. I just thought it would be nice to talk about my father."

She had told me before she met Phil that my father was in medical school when he and my mother got together, but that he died just before he graduated, when I was two years old and Jamie was just a baby. I didn't remember him at all. She had told me it was a car accident. She had said that he'd stayed up all night studying and had gone to classes, then to the hospital for a shift. She had said that he'd fallen asleep at the wheel on his way home. She always said, "At least he was the only one. At least he didn't slam into another car and take someone with him." She seemed to take comfort in that thought. But after she got together with Phil, she never wanted to talk about my father again. She always said, "That's all water under the bridge."

She was still fiddling with the ends of her hair, twirling them around and around her finger, when she looked at me now and said, "That's all water under the bridge, David. It's bad enough having to think that Phil is gone. I don't want to remember any more deaths." Tears welled up in her eyes.

Oh boy, she was going to cry again. "What are we going to do, David?"

I couldn't believe what was happening. And I didn't have an answer to her question.

Chapter Five

Detective Antonelli called the next morning just before I was supposed to leave for school. He asked to speak to my mother. Her hand shook when she took the phone from me. Maybe she thought he was going to tell her that they had caught whoever had shot Phil. By the time she hung up the phone, her hand was shaking even worse and her face was pale.

"He said they want to talk to you, David."

"They?" I said. "The cops?"

She nodded.

"What for?" I don't think I ever worked harder at getting just two words out of my mouth. I tried to sound like I had no idea what the cops would want with me.

"He didn't say," she said. "He just said that they want to talk to you and that it's about Phil. Give me a minute to find my shoes and we'll go."

"You're coming with me?" I said.

"Of course I'm going with you. You're my son."

She found her shoes and her purse and dug out her car keys. We rode in silence. My mother was probably wondering why the cops would want to talk to me about what had happened to Phil. So was I. I told myself over and over that I hadn't done anything. Besides, the cops had told us that no one had seen anything. They had canvassed the whole area. Phil had been killed at a bank machine on a street that had nothing but stores on both sides. They were almost all carpet stores and clothing stores, plus a couple of check-cashing places, a furniture store, a place that sold hats, and a place that sold lamps. All of the stores had been closed at the time. The police hadn't been able to find anyone who had been on that block when it happened. They told my mother that they found a clerk at a convenience store who thought he heard a bang, but who just assumed it was a car backfiring. No one in any of the houses on the streets nearby had heard or seen anything.

Detective Antonelli came out to meet us. He escorted us to an interview room. He started right in telling me that he was investigating Phil's shooting and that he wanted to ask me some questions. He told me that I didn't have to answer his questions, but that if I did answer, anything that I said could be used as evidence against me. My mouth went dry, but the rest of my body got slick with sweat.

"Why are you telling him that?" my mother said. Her voice was higher than normal. It always got shrill when she was upset or mad. "What's going on?"

Detective Antonelli told my mother that he had reason to believe I knew more than I was telling about what had happened to Phil. He told me that I had the right to a lawyer. He told me I could have a lawyer or my mother or any other adult with me while I answered his questions.

"I don't understand," my mother said. "What's going on? You don't think David shot Phil, do you?"

I said I didn't want a lawyer, even though I kind of wished I could have one. But I was afraid to ask for one. I was afraid it would make me look like I had done something. Detective Antonelli told me that if I changed my mind, I should tell him and he would stop asking questions until I had a chance to talk to a lawyer.

"What about your mother, David?" Detective Antonelli said. "Do you want her to stay with you while you answer my questions?"

I looked at my mother. I couldn't decide if I wanted her in the room with me or not.

Finally I said I wanted her to stay.

"David," Detective Antonelli said, "your stepfather was killed at approximately fifteen minutes before midnight on Saturday night. We know that because we have the slip from the ATM machine where he withdrew money. It has the time on it."

I waited. My throat was so dry I thought I would choke.

"You told us that on the night your stepfather was killed, you went out. Is that correct?"

I nodded.

"You said you left the house at 8:00 and that you came back at 10:30. Is that correct?"

I had to force myself not to look at my mother as I nodded again.

"Where did you go, David?"

"I was just walking around."

"Were you with friends?"

I shook my head. "I was by myself. I like to walk around." It was true. I did.

"Where were you walking around?"

Why was he asking me that? Did he already know the answer or was he trying to find out?

"I was just walking around," I said. "Down by First and Main. Around there."

"And you're sure you were home by 10:30 that night?"

My mother was staring at me now. I started to worry about what she might be thinking.

"I'm pretty sure," I said. I didn't want to sound too definite until I knew why he was asking.

"I don't know if you know this, David, but banks have security cameras at their bank machines."

I was pretty sure I had heard that somewhere, but I didn't see what it had to do with me.

"We checked the security video from the bank machine. We saw your stepfather making a withdrawal from his account. But we didn't see anyone else near the bank machine at the same time. We didn't see anyone using the machine just before your stepfather used it or just after either."

Why was he telling me this? What did it have to do with me?

"One of the other things we did, David, to try to find out anything that might help us identify the person who shot your stepfather, is that we collected security surveillance videos from all the businesses in the area. That gave us an idea of who else might have been in the area at the time the crime was committed."

Oh.

Out of the corner of my eye, I saw my mother staring at me. Detective Antonelli was staring at me too, straight in the eye. I wanted to look somewhere else, but I was afraid that if I did, he would think that I had something to hide.

Detective Antonelli said, "David, can you explain why you appear in a surveillance video at a convenience store one block from where your stepfather was shot just ten minutes before it happened?"

Chapter Six

Think fast, I thought to myself.

I said to Detective Antonelli, "Well, I remember I went into a store and bought an ice-cream bar." I said it as calmly as I could, like I was trying to be as helpful as possible.

"You didn't mention that before."

"You didn't ask me," I said. It was true. "I didn't think it was important. It was just ice-cream."

Detective Antonelli gave me a hard look. It scared me.

"Your stepfather was killed at approximately fifteen minutes before midnight, David," he said. "We have you on the security surveillance video in that store at twenty-five minutes to midnight. Yet you told me—you told me *twice* now—that you were home by 10:30. But you weren't. You were at that store at twenty-five minutes to midnight. That means that if you walked home from that store, you couldn't have been home before midnight. That's one and a half hours *later* than what you told us. Why did you lie, David?"

I glanced at my mother. Her face was white. She was staring at me like we were strangers. I looked at Detective Antonelli.

"I'm not supposed to be out that late," I said. "I'm supposed to be home by 11:00 on Saturday night. I didn't want my mom to get mad at me." I turned to her. "I'm sorry I lied, Mom."

"Lying to the police is a serious matter, David," Detective Antonelli said.

"I know. I'm sorry." I didn't even have to pretend. I really was sorry—sorry that he'd found out.

"So now you're saying you *were* in that store approximately ten minutes before your stepfather was shot?" Detective Antonelli said.

"Yes."

"This is an important question, David," Detective Antonelli said.

"Maybe he should have a lawyer," my mother said. That made me feel a little better. Maybe she thought I'd done something wrong, but at least she still cared enough to worry about what was best for me.

"Do you want to call a lawyer, David?" Detective Antonelli said.

I shook my head. "No."

"David, where did you go after you left the store?"

"I went home."

"Which direction did you go in?"

"I walked west."

"On what street?"

47

"Main Street." The bank machine where Phil had been shot was in the other direction.

"Did you hear anything?"

He meant, like a gunshot.

"No," I said.

"Nothing?" he said.

"No."

"Not a gunshot?"

"No."

"You were in the vicinity when your stepfather was shot and you didn't hear anything? Can you explain that, David?"

"No," I said. "Well, except that I walk pretty fast. I was probably all the way down by Second Avenue, maybe even halfway to Third, by the time it must have happened. And I was playing music on my Mp3 player. I play my music pretty loud."

"Did you see anyone while you were walking, David?"

"I don't know. Maybe. Nobody I knew."

"Nobody who could confirm where you say you were?"

"I don't know," I said.

Detective Antonelli stared at me again for a few moments.

"How well did you get along with your stepfather, David?" he said.

He thought I'd done it. He thought I was the one who had shot Phil. Why else would he ask me that question?

"He was okay," I said.

"That's not what we heard," Detective Antonelli said. "We heard that you and your stepfather argued a lot."

"Well, yeah," I said. "Most guys I know argue with their parents. But that doesn't mean they go out and shoot them."

"What kind of things did you argue about?"

I shrugged. "Regular stuff," I said. "Chores. Curfews. Homework." Mostly what happened was that my mother complained to Phil on the weekend about something I'd done during the week while he was on the road, and Phil yelled at me about it. Or Phil had a bunch of chores that he wanted me to do, and I got mad because he was mostly never home, and the minute he got

home he was like the evil stepmother—
Cinderella, do this. Cinderella, do that. And
I was Cinderella.

"Did he ever hit you?"

"*What*?" Phil was a jerk, but he wasn't
that kind of a jerk. "No."

Detective Antonelli looked at my mother
for confirmation. My mother's face was
tense. She looked at him, biting her lip.
Chewing on it, really. She opened her purse
and fumbled in it. I thought she was going
for a tissue. She wasn't. She pulled out
something and set it on the table in front of
her. It was the gold-framed picture of my
brother that used to be on Phil's key chain.

"This is the item I told you about," she
said to Detective Antonelli. "The item that
my husband usually carried with him but
that was missing from his things after he
was…" Her voice trembled. "After he died,"
she said finally. She took a deep breath. "I
found it in the clothes dryer when I was
taking clothes out of it. They were all
David's clothes, including the clothes he
was wearing on Saturday night."

Geez, my own mother! What was she doing?

She turned to me. "Tell Detective Antonelli what you did, David. Tell him and tell me."

Chapter Seven

Detective Antonelli looked at my mother for a moment. Then he looked at me. He said, "Do you want a lawyer present, David?"

"No," I said. "But—" I glanced at my mother. "I want to talk to you in private," I said. "I don't want my mother here."

I had a pretty good idea how my mother must have felt when I said that. I was sure she was thinking the worst. But I didn't care. I didn't want her there.

She didn't want to leave.

"I'm his mother," she said to Detective Antonelli. "I have the right to be here."

Detective Antonelli stared at me. "Are you sure, David?" he said. "You have the right to have a parent here in the room with you."

"I'm sure," I said.

"Do you want another adult here with you?"

"No."

"I'm staying," my mother said. "You can't talk to my son without me present."

Detective Antonelli stood up. He said, "May I speak to you outside for a minute, Mrs. Benson?"

It took my mother a moment before she got to her feet and followed him out of the room. Five minutes passed. When the door to the interview room opened again, Detective Antonelli came in alone.

"Your mother is waiting for you outside," he said. "David, you have decided not to have a parent or any adult present with you. Is that right?"

"Yes."

"If at any time you change your mind about that, tell me. I will stop asking you questions until you have been able to talk to your parent or to another adult and, if you want, to have that person here with you. Do you understand?"

"Yes," I said and then asked, "My mother can't see me, can she?" I looked at the mirror on the wall and wondered if she was on the other side, watching.

"No," Detective Antonelli said.

"She can't hear what I'm saying?"

"No, she can't."

I looked at him, but I couldn't tell what he was thinking. I didn't know him well enough. Besides, he was a cop. Cops have a special way of talking and looking.

"How do I know?" I said.

"You have my word, David. Your mother can't hear what you're saying and she can't see you. I'm being truthful with you, David. Why don't you be truthful with me? Tell me about your stepfather."

"He liked to gamble. He liked to play poker."

"That's not what I mean, David."

"This is important," I said. "I can tell it my way, right?"

Detective Antonelli's eyes were dark and sharp. He never took them off me when he was talking to me or when I was talking to him. He didn't take them off me now as he leaned back in his chair and said, "Yes, you can tell it your way."

So I told him about Phil and how much he liked poker. He liked it so much that whenever he told me to do something and I didn't want to do it, he always said, "Tell you what. Let the cards decide. We'll play a hand of five-card draw."

If Phil won, I had to do whatever stupid chore he had in mind for me. If he lost, he didn't necessarily have to do it instead, but neither did I. Sometimes, "just to keep it interesting," as Phil would say, we played best two out of three.

I gave Detective Antonelli an example.

About two weeks earlier, my mother went into the garage to try to find something that she had brought with her when she and Jamie and I had moved into Phil's place a little over six years ago. I couldn't remember what she was looking for. I'm not even sure she told me what it was. But I do remember that she couldn't find it and that she said it was because the garage was such a mess. It was piled with stuff that, according to her, she hadn't seen Phil use even once since we'd moved in. She muttered about it all week. She said that when Phil came home for the weekend, if he did one thing and one thing only, he was going to clean out the garage.

When Phil came home that weekend—one week before he got shot at the bank machine—they had an argument about the garage. Phil said what he always said: "I'm away from my family all week, working hard to put food on the table, a roof over everyone's head, clothes on everyone's back. When I come home for the weekend, I expect to relax. I *deserve* to relax."

But my mother didn't back down. She wanted the garage cleaned out.

No way, Phil told her. It was a whole-weekend job, and if she thought he was going to spend the whole weekend doing chores after he'd just spent the whole week working, she was going to have to think again.

My mother still didn't back down. She was here all week, she said. She had to look at that mess. Worse, she had to try to find stuff in that mess. And, by the way, she told Phil, "I work too. I put in twenty-five hours a week at the store. Plus I keep this house clean. I take care of all the details. I make sure there's food in the fridge and in the freezer so that you can eat good home-cooked meals when you're here." My mother was a good cook. "I make sure there are clean clothes in your closet and clean socks and underwear in your drawers. I even do beer runs so that there'll be plenty on hand when your friends come over."

Phil didn't say anything to that. Instead, he looked at me. He said, "David, I've got a little job for you."

"No way," I said. None of the stuff in the garage belonged to me. I didn't see why I should have to clean it out.

"I'll play you for it," Phil said.

It was such a big job that I wasn't sure I wanted to play him. I didn't want to take the chance I'd lose.

My mother said, "One of you is going to clean the garage or neither of you is going to get a meal out of me for a month." It was totally unfair. I was the one who would suffer the most if she refused to cook. Phil was away five days out of seven. She scowled at us and left the kitchen.

"Come on, Davy," Phil said, needling me. He knew I didn't like to be called that. "We'll play best two out of three."

"Okay," I said. I knew my mother wasn't bluffing. She was angry about the garage and she wanted the job done. "On one condition."

Phil looked at me. "Now you're giving me conditions?"

"It's for Mom," I said. "The loser *has* to clean out the garage, even if it's you. Deal?"

Phil thought for a moment. "Deal," he said. He stuck out his hand and we shook.

Phil dealt the cards. I won the first hand—a pair of queens to his pair of nines. Phil won the next hand—three jacks to my pair of fives and pair of sevens. The next hand was the one that would decide whose weekend was ruined. I discarded three and tried to keep from grinning when I picked up the three replacements that Phil dealt me. One of them was a king. I added it to the two kings I already had in my hand. I was picturing Phil cleaning out the garage when there was a knock on the back door. The door opened and Jack appeared in the kitchen. "Hey," he said when he saw us, "I thought the game was tonight."

"It is," I said. "We're just playing a couple of hands to see who has to clean out the garage."

"Talk about high-stakes poker," Jack said with a laugh. He went to the fridge and pulled out a beer. He was watching us the whole time.

Phil discarded four cards—I definitely had him. I didn't bother trying to keep a poker face now. He drew four from the deck.

"Read 'em and weep," I said, throwing down my cards. There were my three kings staring up at Phil.

Phil turned over his cards. Four aces. I couldn't believe it.

"Looks like someone has his weekend cut out for him," Phil said, grinning as he collected the cards from the table. "You ready to go to the car show, Jack?"

I slapped the table with one hand. Damn! I glanced at Jack. He shook his head.

"Is that why you did it?" Detective Antonelli said. "Because you lost and you were mad at your stepfather? Because you had to spend the weekend cleaning up *his* garage?"

I told him, "You don't understand. I didn't do it."

Chapter Eight

"You said I could tell it my way," I said to Detective Antonelli.

"You can, David," he said. "But I'd like you to stick to the point, okay?"

"I am," I said.

So I told him what happened next.

Phil was still grinning after he gathered the cards and got up from the table. He said to Jack, "I have to go upstairs and change my shirt and grab my wallet. I'll be with you in a minute."

Jack told him to take his time. He leaned on the counter, working on the beer he'd taken from the fridge.

"Do you guys do that a lot?" he said.

"Do what?" I said. "Play cards?"

"Play for stuff," Jack said.

I nodded. Jack took another pull of beer.

"What do you play for?" he said.

"Chores, mostly. Stupid stuff, like cleaning out the garbage cans or taking the empties back to the beer store. And big stuff too. Like shoveling the driveway after a major storm. Or, one time, painting the downstairs bathroom with Mom."

"And today?"

"Today it was cleaning out the garage. It's going to take me all weekend."

Jack looked thoughtful as he sipped more beer.

"Is the split pretty much even?" Jack said.

"What do you mean?"

"I mean, does Phil win maybe half the time and you win the other half?"

I thought about it. "He wins way more often than I do," I said. I thought about it some more. "When it's really big stuff, like today, he almost always wins," I said. I looked at Jack. I was pretty sure he was going to say something else, but just then Phil came back and the two of them took off.

I spent the whole day cleaning out the garage. Then, because I didn't want to spend all day Sunday working on it too, I decided to work right through and finish the whole thing on Saturday night, no matter how long it took. I was making pretty good progress. By 10:00, all I had left to do was take out the bags of garbage and sweep the garage floor. I'd cleaned it up so well that Phil could even park his car in the garage now if he wanted to. He hadn't been able to do that for as long as my mother and I had been living there.

I took a quick break and went into the house to get a soda from the fridge. Phil and Jack and a bunch of Phil's friends were sitting around the dining room table, playing poker. When Phil heard me come into the kitchen, he called for me to bring him a cold beer. He asked around the table and said, "Make that five cold ones, Davy."

I brought in the beers just in time to see Jack put down his cards. Phil groaned and threw his cards into the middle of the table. Jack grinned and raked in all the chips. He took a long drink from the cold beer I handed him.

"What do you say we take a break?" one of the other guys said. He was a smoker and my mother didn't allow smoking in the house. Phil went along with it even though I bet he used to smoke his cigars in the house before we moved in. The three guys who did smoke went outside. Phil pulled out a cigar and went with them. I went back through the kitchen and into the garage. Jack followed me.

"How's the job going, David?" he said. Then he stepped into the garage. "Wow!"

he said. "I didn't know this place even had a floor. You must have worked your butt off all day."

He had that right.

"Who's winning?" I said.

"The night's still young," Jack said. "Things could change."

"Yeah, but right now, who's ahead?"

"I am."

"And Phil?" I asked.

"I guess you could say he's not doing so well."

Just like always. I'd hung around more than a few of their games over the years, a lot of times running beers for them and refilling bowls of chips and pretzels. Sometimes I ordered pizza for them and brought it in with paper plates and napkins.

"I guess that's because you've been playing serious poker for a long time," I said.

"What do you mean?" Jack said.

"I mean, you have way more experience with cards than me. When Phil plays me, he wins more than he loses." I'd been thinking about that all afternoon. If it was something really big that had to get done in order to stop my mother from having a meltdown, I always lost. If it was something small that Phil could just decide not to do, I sometimes won. "But when he plays you, he usually loses more than he wins, and when he wins, he doesn't win big. Or maybe he's just lucky with me and not so lucky with you."

Jack glanced back over his shoulder into the kitchen. He closed the door. He said, "If I tell you something, you have to promise to keep it to yourself, okay, David?"

I nodded.

"I guess you could say in a way that I win more because I have more experience," he said. "But not in the way you mean. Phil has a tough time playing against me because I have a tell on him."

"A tell?" I said. "What do you mean?"

"In poker, a tell is any kind of gesture or mannerism that gives you some idea of how good or bad a person's hand is," Jack said. "For example, if you see a player constantly looking at his hole cards, that's often a tell of a poor hand. Of course, some players know that, so they check their hole cards a lot even when they have a great hand, just to throw you off. Another example is that some people play with their chips every time they bluff without even realizing it. Some blink a lot more than usual when they have a strong hand. If you pay attention, you can pick up tells on people. It can give you an edge."

"And you have a tell on Phil?"

Jack nodded.

"What is it?"

Jack shook his head. "I can't tell you that. But if you watch him, maybe you can figure it out." He studied me for a few minutes. "Phil is pretty consistent," he said. "It doesn't matter if he's playing poker or he's doing something else, you can always tell when he's not on the level."

"You mean, when he's bluffing?" I said.

Jack nodded. "Or when he's doing something that maybe he shouldn't. Or being untruthful." I noticed he didn't come right out and say cheating or lying. "But if you want to figure out what his tell is, you have to watch him closely."

"And that's why he beats me so much?"

Jack looked around the garage, like maybe he was hoping to find something. Finally he shook his head.

"Next time you watch him play poker with me and the other guys, watch what he does with his cards at the end of a hand," he said.

"What do you mean?"

"Just watch. And then watch what he does with his cards when he plays hands with you."

Detective Antonelli shifted in his chair.

"David," he said. "I already asked you once to stick to the point."

"I am sticking to the point," I said.

"Okay. So now I'm going to ask you get to the point."

I told him, "Wait."

Chapter Nine

I didn't finish cleaning the garage that night after all. Instead I went inside and fetched beers for Phil and his friends. Besides Jack there was Ted, Mike and Arnie. Except for Jack, they were all truckers. I kept the chip bowl and the pretzel bowl filled to the brim. I ordered the pizza when they got hungry for something bigger and greasier. And I watched Phil play poker.

At first it was confusing. I didn't know what I was looking for. I didn't think I'd ever figure it out. I watched Phil win hands and lose hands. I watched him fold sometimes before a hand was played out. He did a lot of things when he played. They all did. They munched handfuls of pretzels. They fiddled with their poker chips. They swigged beer. They ran their fingers through their hair. They scratched themselves all kinds of places. Maybe some of it meant something. Maybe it didn't.

Then came a hand where Phil bet big. Ted laughed.

"Phil's bluffing again," he said. He raised Phil's bet.

I glanced at Jack. He was looking at Phil as if he was the only person in the room. He was staring at him, hard. So I looked at Phil too. When I did, I saw him do something that made me almost fall over, as if someone had just kicked me hard in the gut and all the wind had come out of me. After that I couldn't take my eyes off him.

Mike studied Phil for a minute.

"Face it, Phil," he said. "It's not your night, and the bluffing isn't going to help."

Phil matched Ted's bet. Then he said, "Hell, might as well make it interesting." He raised and then he looked at Arnie, who did the same thing.

Then it was Jack's turn. He said, "Fold," and threw down his cards.

Phil laughed and raised again.

Ted looked at Jack and folded.

"Wuss," said Mike. He called. So did Arnie.

Phil won with a straight flush, king high.

"Damn," Mike said. "I could have sworn you were bluffing again."

I glanced at Jack. He had known that Phil had a strong hand this time. I was positive he had. And I was pretty sure I knew how he knew.

I hung around for the rest of the game. For a while I wasn't really paying attention. I was too stunned by what I had seen. I was remembering so much that I started to feel like Phil's garage before I'd cleaned it. There were so many memories and they were all about to cascade down around me and bury me.

When the game finally broke up, everyone was talking and fooling around and I couldn't get Jack alone. Finally everyone left. I hurried to catch up with Jack, who was on his way to his pickup.

"Hey, where are you going?" Phil said when I bolted out the door. "You're supposed to be helping me tidy up."

"I'll be back in a minute," I called to him, even though I had already decided that I wasn't going to help him with anything ever again.

I caught up with Jack just as he was slipping the key into the ignition. He opened his window.

"You knew he wasn't bluffing," I said. "You knew it."

Jack didn't say anything.

"It was his face, wasn't it? Before, he was watching everything that was happening. He was really paying attention.

But when he pulled some good cards, all of a sudden he had a blank look on his face, like he didn't care anymore, like whatever. And his lips." I had noticed that right away. "He licked his lips a couple of times, right?"

"With Phil, mostly it's the lips," Jack said. He grinned at me. "You should take up poker. You're pretty observant."

There was also the other thing Jack had told me to watch for. He said I should look at what Phil did with his cards at the end of a hand when he was playing with Jack and when he was playing with me. I had done exactly what Jack had said.

"At the end of a hand with you, Phil throws his cards onto the pile where all the other cards are," I said. "With me, he puts his hands over the cards and he slides them in to where my cards are and then he sort of blends them in with the rest of the deck."

Jack didn't say anything.

"What does it mean, Jack?"

"What does what mean?" Jack said.

"He puts his hands over the cards when he plays with me."

"Covers them up, you mean," Jack said.

I nodded.

"Like maybe he's hiding something," Jack said. He turned the key in the ignition. "I know he's your dad, David—"

"He's my stepfather."

Jack shrugged. "It's not my family. It's none of my business. I shouldn't get involved."

I waited.

"But some things are wrong," he said. "And I can't just stand back and watch them happen. That's why I told you what to look for."

Maybe that's where Jack was different from me, but I didn't say anything. Instead I went back inside. I looked at the mess in the living room. There were empty beer bottles everywhere. And ground-up potato chips and pretzels all over the carpet. Plus dirty paper plates and napkins, dirty glasses, and some pizza grease stains on the table that my mother would freak over if she ever saw them, because this was her table—or so she always said. She had picked it out. Phil had probably paid for it. She always made a big deal over using coasters and place mats so that the table wouldn't get marked up.

"Come on," Phil said. "Help me tidy up."

"I just spent all night cleaning the garage," I said. "You tidy up."

I knew that Phil was angry because his face got all red.

"I'll play you for it," he said. "If you lose, you do the cleanup by yourself."

"Two out of three," I said so I'd have a good chance to watch.

I won the first hand. I didn't see Phil do anything out of the ordinary. At the end of the hand, he threw his cards in.

On the second hand, Phil licked his lips when he fanned out his cards and again after picking up three cards. He won that hand. He slid his cards in.

The same thing happened on the third hand. Phil licked his lips. I don't think he even noticed he was doing it. He won again.

"I guess that settles it," he said.

He started to slide his cards into the middle. I reached out and pushed his hand away from the cards. I guess he didn't expect that because he looked startled. I grabbed his cards before he could react. He tried to snatch them back, but I got up from the table and ran into the kitchen.

I had started with five cards. I'd discarded three and drawn three more. When the hand was over, I threw my cards onto the discard pile. Phil had also started with five cards. He had also discarded three and thrown them onto the discard pile. So there should only have been five cards under his hand as he slid them across the table. But instead there were eight—the five that made up his winning hand and that he had showed me, and three more. Where had the extra three cards come from? There was only one explanation.

Phil came into the kitchen. He glanced at the cards in my hand. I stared at him.

"You cheated," I said.

He didn't say anything.

"All this time you've been playing hands with me, you've been cheating."

He tried to laugh it off. "It's not like I was stealing from you, Davy," he said. "It's not like we were playing for money."

"You cheated," I said again. I couldn't believe it. Well, maybe that wasn't exactly true. Maybe it wasn't a huge surprise to me that Phil would do something like that. But I felt like an idiot for being cheated by him all this time and never knowing it. "I'm going to tell Mom," I said. I probably sounded like a baby saying that, but I wanted her to know what kind of jerk she had married.

"She won't believe you," Phil said. "Not after I talk to her. That's the trouble with being a pain in the ass, Davy. She knows you don't like me. She knows you never listen to me. Now, as far as she's concerned, you're just going to kick it up a notch and start telling lies about me. Keep it up and nobody's going to be sorry when you're finally old enough to move out."

I looked at Detective Antonelli.

"Is that why you did it, David?" he said. "Because you found out that your stepfather was cheating you at cards?"

"I didn't do it," I told him. "I didn't do anything." And, boy, that was the truth.

Chapter Ten

Detective Antonelli stared at me. He said, "Where did you get the gun?"

"What gun?"

"Come on, David," he said. "Your stepfather was shot dead. Your mother found the missing picture of your brother in the clothes dryer. Your clothes were the only ones in the dryer. We know for a fact that you were in the immediate area right before your stepfather was shot.

And you lied to us about it. Where did you get the gun? What did you do with it afterward?"

"I never had a gun. I didn't do it," I told him again.

Detective Antonelli looked impatient.

"I just told you about Phil cheating so you'd get an idea what kind of person he was," I said. "The important part has to do with that hand he played with Jack. The one where he kept raising and he won, and where Jack folded."

"What about it, David?" Detective Antonelli said. He sounded worse than impatient. He sounded annoyed.

"I saw what Jack was talking about," I said. "I figured out what Phil's tell was. After he looked at his cards, just before he bet, when Jack was looking at him, *studying* him"—I wanted him to get that part—"Phil's face changed. One minute he was right in there, watching everything. Then, just like that, he licked his lips and his eyes went kind of blank, like he was trying hard not to show what he was really feeling, like he didn't want everyone to know he had a great hand for a change."

"David, we need to get back on topic here."

"Do you remember what my mother told you about my brother Jamie?" I said.

"David—"

"Do you?"

"She said he drowned."

"We were at this cottage that Phil had borrowed from a friend of his," I said. "We were supposed to spend two weeks there. My mom was nervous about it. She never learned to swim. She didn't like the water. Jamie didn't know how to swim either. Mom tried to make him go to swimming lessons, but he horsed around so much all the time that they kicked him out. She made him wear a life jacket just to go on the beach, and she made sure that either she or Phil was watching him all the time. Phil, he could swim. He always boasted how he was on the swim team in high school. He has a bunch of medals and ribbons in a display case on the wall of his study." They were probably the only things he had ever won. He was probably one of those guys whose best years were in high school.

"And you?" Detective Antonelli said.

"I took swimming lessons in school. My swimming instructor said I was a better swimmer than any ten-year-old he had ever seen."

Detective Antonelli said, "This is going somewhere, right, David?"

I said it was. I told him how broken up my mother had been when Jamie drowned.

"If he was wearing a life jacket, how did he drown?" Detective Antonelli said.

"That's the thing," I said. "Jamie never listened. Or if he did, he listened to what you told him to do and then he did the opposite. He was going out in the boat with Phil. The boat belonged to the same guy who let Phil have the cottage. It had a big outboard motor on it. They were out there together—Phil and Jamie. It was my mother's idea. You know, let them have a little quality time together and maybe

Phil would warm up to Jamie, and Jamie would listen to Phil for a change. I was on the shore. I could see them. They weren't out all that far. Phil had paddled out to where the water was deep and he wanted to start the engine. I could see that Jamie didn't have his life jacket on."

"David, I'm sorry about your brother," Detective Antonelli said. "But unless this has something to do—"

"I think my mother liked that Phil carried Jamie's picture around with him all the time," I said. "I think that made her believe that Phil really loved Jamie. It sure made everyone else believe it. People were always telling Phil what a good guy he was, but how maybe he made it hard on himself, having that picture with him all the time. He got a lot of sympathy from it. One time he told me he got a lot of free drinks too, you know, from people who would see the picture on his key chain and say, Is that your son? And then he'd tell them the whole story." Well, he didn't tell the *whole* story. He told his version of it. "And people would feel sorry for him and buy him a beer."

Someone knocked on the door to the interview room. It was a cop. He said, "The mother wants to be in here with her son. She's making a big fuss about it. She says she's going to call a lawyer."

Detective Antonelli sighed and looked at me.

"She can come in if she wants," I said. "But first I want to tell you about my brother Jamie."

"After that you'll tell about your stepfather?"

I said I would. Then I told him about Jamie. I told him a few other things too. After he listened, he sent another cop to check on some of what I said. When the other cop finally came back into the room, he said something to Detective Antonelli in a quiet voice that I couldn't hear. Detective Antonelli said, "Show Mrs. Benson in."

Chapter Eleven

When my mother came back into the room, her eyes were pink and swollen. She had been crying. But her lipstick and mascara looked just fine, so I figured she must have done a repair job in the bathroom. The little gold-framed picture of Jamie still sat in the middle of the table. My mother seemed startled to see it there. Maybe she thought it should have been taken away as evidence.

"Please sit down, Mrs. Benson," Detective Antonelli said.

She sat down next to me, but didn't look at me. She didn't ask me how I was either.

Detective Antonelli said, "Mrs. Benson, do you think that what happened to your husband had anything at all to do with your son's death?"

My mother looked even more startled.

"I don't see how," she said. "Jamie's death was an accident." Her hand went to her hair, and she started to fiddle with the ends of it.

Detective Antonelli looked at her for a few moments. Then he glanced at me. I couldn't tell what he was thinking. But cops are supposed to be good at that. They're supposed to be good at not revealing things. I wondered if they were also good poker players.

"Do you think that you'd like to contact David's father?" he said. "His real father, I mean?"

"David's real father is dead," my mother said. She continued to fiddle with her hair.

"He died in a car accident when David was barely two years old."

"What about Jamie's father?" Detective Antonelli said.

My mother glanced at me. She was twirling hair around one of her fingers now. I wondered if she even knew she was doing it.

"I don't understand," she said.

"David has something to say," Detective Antonelli said.

My mother turned her head slowly to look at me. Her eyes were wide and scared-looking. "So it's true," she said. "You did have something to do with it. What did you do, David? Why did you do it? You have to tell."

So I did.

I didn't look at Detective Antonelli when I told. I looked at my mother. And I didn't talk about Phil, not directly anyway. I talked about Jamie. I told her about the day he drowned.

"Phil was irritated with him, remember?" I said.

"Why are you talking about this?" my mother said. "I don't want to think about that. It was a horrible accident."

"Phil was pissed off and you said maybe, if he took Jamie out in the boat, it would be good for both of them. You didn't want me to go. You said it was just Jamie and Phil. And I got mad. Remember?"

My mother looked at Detective Antonelli.

"I remember," she said. "But—"

"Phil paddled the boat out to where the water was deep and then he tried to start it. Jamie didn't have his life jacket on. Phil told you that later. Remember?"

My mother's face was pale. She nodded.

"You were sleeping on the dock, remember? And Jamie was acting crazy in the boat. Phil yelled at him. He told him if he wasn't careful, he was going to fall in the water. Remember?"

"I was asleep, David. I didn't hear that." She looked at me closely. "And you weren't even there. You were up in the cottage. You didn't come down until after."

What she meant was I didn't come down until she screamed. But she was wrong.

"When I got mad because you wouldn't let me go in the boat with Phil and Jamie, you told me to go up to the cottage. You said to have a time-out in my room. But I didn't. Instead I snuck back down and hid under the canoe on the beach. Remember that canoe, Mom? It was upside down on the sand?"

Her face turned even paler.

"I saw them. Phil warned Jamie. Jamie was standing up in the boat without his life jacket on. Phil started the boat and it lurched. Jamie fell overboard. He was splashing around. He yelled. You remember him yelling, don't you?"

I knew she did because Jamie's yell had woken her up. She'd sat up and put her hands over her eyes to block the sun. As soon as she saw that Jamie was in the water, she ran to the end of the dock and started screaming.

"Phil was just sitting there, remember? He was sitting in the boat like he was frozen and you screamed at him to help Jamie. But he didn't move. Remember?"

"I can't swim," my mother said quietly to Detective Antonelli. Tears welled up in her eyes.

"And I ran into the water," I said. "Remember? I tried to swim to Jamie, but by the time I got there, he wasn't there anymore." By the time I got to him, he was underwater. "I dove to get him. I heard you screaming again."

"I thought you were going to drown too," she said.

"And then Phil jumped into the water. He pulled me up and then he went down for Jamie. Remember? And he was down there a long time." Maybe he was down there as long as he was because it took that long to find Jamie. Or maybe he was down there so long because he just wanted to make it look like he was trying. "And by the time he brought Jamie up—"

"Stop!" my mother said. "Stop. Why are you talking about this? What does this have to do with what happened to Phil?"

"Jamie wasn't breathing," I said. "Phil dragged him to the shore and got out of the water. He was just standing there with Jamie in his arms. Do you remember what he said, Mom?"

I did. I remembered perfectly. I'd seen it in my dreams a thousand times or more. "He said that he was so stunned by what happened that he just froze out there in the boat. That's why he didn't jump in the water right away. He said he just froze. Remember?" *I* remembered. He licked his lips a couple of times and his face changed and he said, *I froze.* "And I made him put Jamie down and I tried to do mouth-to-mouth on him." I had learned a little of that from my swimming lessons. "Phil said it was too late. And you started to cry. Phil finally called 911. And when they came, there was nothing they could do because Jamie had drowned."

"It was an accident," my mother said. She kept touching her hair. I'd seen that before too. She did it when she talked about my real father. She did it when she talked about Jamie. And she did it that day on the dock when she told me, "It was an accident, David. It was a terrible accident. We have to be strong. It was terrible what happened to Jamie, but we have to think about Phil too. About how he must feel." She said, "No matter what anyone might say or do, nothing can bring Jamie back to us." She said, "We can't blame Phil for what happened. People react in funny ways." She said, "David, I don't know what we would do without Phil."

"It was an accident that Jamie fell into the water," I said to her. "But it wasn't an accident he drowned, was it, Mom?"

My mother was crying. Crying and fiddling with her hair. "Why are you saying this?" she said. "Why are you talking about this? It was an accident."

"Phil could have saved him," I said. "Phil was right there. He was a good swimmer. He could have saved Jamie, but instead he did nothing. And then he lied about it. And you knew he was lying."

"No," my mother said. "That's not true."

"Yes, it is, Mom. I know it is." I knew because I knew her tell. Phil licked his lips and got a blank look in his eyes. My mother fiddled with her hair. "I also know that you lied about my real father. I know he isn't dead." Jack had told I. "And I know that Jamie and I don't have the same father." Jack had told me that too. Jack was a good guy. He thought it was wrong for Phil to cheat me and wrong for my mother to lie to me. He said he knew where my father was and that, if I wanted, he could tell me how to contact him. I wasn't sure I wanted to.

My mother stared at me. Detective Antonelli looked at her. He had watched her play with her hair when she talked about Jamie, just like she had when she'd talked about my father. And he knew that my mother had lied about my father because he had checked with Jack before he let her back into the room.

Chapter Twelve

A police officer escorted my mother out of the room. After she was gone, Detective Antonelli said, "Is that why you killed your stepfather, David? Because he could have saved Jamie, but he didn't?"

"I didn't kill him," I said. "I swear I didn't."

Detective Antonelli waited. So finally I told him the truth.

The truth was that it was a coincidence that I happened to see Phil at the bank machine that night. I had gone for a walk, just like I said. I had stopped and bought an ice-cream bar, and I was just about to head home when I saw Phil. I ducked back out of sight because I didn't want him to see me. I had a curfew, and if he caught me out after it, he'd tell my mother and she'd be all over me.

"I ducked into the doorway of a store that was closed," I said. "I was in the shadows, you know, so I figured he couldn't see me. Then I watched so I could see when he was gone and maybe which direction he was going in." I'd been hoping he wouldn't jump in his car and drive straight home and find out I wasn't there.

"Then I saw this guy come up to him and say something to him. Phil said something back. I saw him shake his head. The guy said something else. Phil shoved him away and swore at him. He turned away from the guy. Then I saw the guy take out a gun. He pointed it at Phil. I knew he was going to shoot. I thought about yelling something, but I was afraid the guy might shoot at me instead. The guy said something to Phil. Phil turned. The guy shot him."

I'd been stunned. I could see it was going to happen, and at the same time I couldn't believe it actually would.

"Then the guy took his wallet and ran away."

"Did you see him before he ran?" Detective Antonelli said.

I nodded.

"Could you identify him, David?"

I said I probably could. I said I could probably describe him pretty well too. And that was the truth. His face was burned into my brain.

"I ran over to where Phil was," I said. "He was breathing, but he was also making a sort of gurgling sound. He looked at me. But I just stood there. I couldn't move. He had his keys in his hands, and I saw that picture of my brother and thought about Phil, with his display case full of swimming medals and ribbons, just sitting in that boat while Jamie drowned." I also thought about his face when he told my mother that he had frozen. I thought about him licking his lips when he told the paramedics and the cops the same thing. I thought about him waving that key chain under everyone's nose and telling them his son had drowned. I remembered all the free beers he got when he told people about Jamie. "Then Phil stopped making that noise. He stopped everything. I grabbed his keys and I ran. I broke the chain and took Jamie's picture, and I threw the keys away. Then I went home."

Detective Antonelli was quiet for a minute. Then he said, "The pathologist said he was shot through the heart, David, and that he died within a minute or two. He said that even if the paramedics had arrived in three minutes, they wouldn't have been able to do anything. He would have been dead already."

It took them nearly a month, but they finally caught the guy who shot Phil. They did it based on my description, and when they brought him in, they asked me to identify him. I don't have to go to court because the guy made a deal with the prosecutor. He got life for second-degree murder but is eligible for parole in fifteen years, which means he could get out in eight. My mother cried when she heard that.

Jack doesn't come around as much as he used to, and my mother doesn't talk about him. I think she's mad at him for telling me about my dad. I still haven't decided what to do about him. I'm curious, but not that curious. After all, it's not like he ever came looking for me.

And about Phil—I tell myself I didn't do anything wrong. Phil would have died anyway. But I didn't know that at the time. At the time, I just looked at him and remembered him licking his lips and remembered his face going blank when he told my mother there was nothing he could have done about Jamie. That's why I didn't call an ambulance for him. That's why I didn't do anything except stand there. In those few minutes, I did what Phil had done. I *became* Phil. I hate myself for that. But I know that I will never be Phil again. Not in a million years.

My mother still doesn't know what she's going to do without him—or *with* me.

Norah McClintock has been writing compelling fiction for years. *Tell* is her second Orca Soundings novel. *Snitch*, an ALA Popular Paperback, was published in 2005.

Other titles in the
Orca Soundings series

Other titles in the
Orca Soundings series

Visit www.orcabook.com for more information.

More Orca Soundings

Exit Point
by Laura Langston

"I'm not dead. I'm still me. I still have a body and everything."

"You are still you, but you don't have a body. What you're seeing is a thought form." He points to a tall gold urn up by the minister. "Your body is in there. You were cremated."

Thunk thunk, thunk thunk. My heart pounds in my chest. Dread mushrooms in my stomach. Sweat beads on my forehead. "But everybody knows death is the end. That there's nothing left but matter."

"Death is only the beginning, Logan. Hannah knows that. Lots of people do."

Logan always takes the easy way out. After a night of drinking and driving, he wakes up to find he has been involved in a car accident and is dead. With the help of his guide, Wade, and the spirit of his grandmother, he realizes he has taken the wrong exit. He wasn't meant to die. His life had a purpose—to save his sister!

Exposure
by Patricia Murdoch

I was happier than I had been for a long time. Everything was crashing down around Dana. Finally I was getting some justice. But I wanted a bigger helping. This wasn't enough. I had to do something.

I went into the washroom and dug a marker out of my pencil case. I drew a box and a couple of circles, with lines for a flash going off, on the outer wall of the first cubicle. No one would be able to miss it. It didn't look exactly like a camera, but it would do. And for the finishing touch I wrote SMILE DANA, with a happy face right beside it.

More Orca Soundings

Stuffed
by Eric Walters

"So, do we have a deal?" Mr. Evans asked.

"Unbelievable," I muttered under my breath.

"I don't understand," Mr. Evans said.

"The whole thing is unbelievable. First you try to threaten me. Then you try to bribe me. And now you do the two together, trying to bribe me and threatening me if I don't take the bribe."

"I don't like to think of it in those terms," he said.

When Ian and his classmates watch a documentary about the health concerns of eating fast food, Ian decides to start a boycott against a multinational food chain. Can Ian stand up for what he believes in? Can he take on a corporate behemoth and win?